BURN THE FIELD

poems by

Amy Beeder

Carnegie Mellon University Press

Pittsburgh 2006

ACKNOWLEDGMENTS

Grateful acknowledgment is made to the editors of the following magazines in which these poems first appeared:

AGNI: "Train"
American Letters & Commentary: "Humbug"
Beloit Poetry Journal: "Cotton & Turnip," "Western City"
Black Warrior Review: "Photograph in a Montana Bar"
Boulevard: "Last Photo"
Connecticut Review: "Cockfight," "Sonnet for an Early Thaw," "Drowning in Bosporus"
Fine Madness: "Cured"
Margie: The American Journal of Poetry: "Lost Jockey," "Photo of Pasteur"
The Nation: "Rooster Shadow"
Painted Bride Quarterly: "Blanca"
Pleiades: "Frozen Charlotte," "Zuckerman's Daughter"
Poetry: "Cabezón," "The Deadly Poppy Field," "Vertigo," "Mumbletypeg," "Fever," "Two Poems After Ovid," "Yellow Dress"
Poetry Daily: "The Deadly Poppy Field"
Poetry East: "What Children Do in the Ravine"
Post Road: "Botany Notes," "No Child Will Choose It"
Prairie Schooner: "On Preferring Red or Black Dates," "Scent"
Puerto del Sol: "From Vacant Lots, Flowers . . ."
River Styx: "Wrought"
Salt Hill: "Gunslinger"
Spoon River Poetry Review: "On Two Paintings by Narcisse Virgil Diaz de la Pena," "The Body's Luck"
Witness: "Hangman," "Again, the Donkey"

Cover image from *Das Kleine Buch Der Tropenwunder* by Maria Sibylla Merian

The publication of this book is supported by a grant from the Pennsylvania Council on the Arts.

Library of Congress Control Number: 2005924484
ISBN- 13: 978-0-88748-448-3
ISBN- 10: 0-88748-448-4

Printed and bound in the United States of America

10 9 8 7 6 5 4 3 2 1

Burn the Field

CONTENTS

I

The Deadly Poppy Field 9
Cabezón 10
Photograph in a Montana Bar 11
From Vacant Lots, Flowers . . . 12
Humbug 13
Rooster Shadow 14
Cotton & Turnip 15
Again, the Donkey 16
Train 18
Scent 20
Hangman 21
Photo of Pasteur 22
On Two Paintings
by Narcisse Virgil Diaz de la Peña 23
Varicose 25
Vertigo 26
Gunslinger 28
On Preferring Red or Black Dates 29

II

Zuckerman's Daughter 33
Sonnet for an Early Thaw 35
Mother as a House 36

Croup 38
The Cockfight 39
Fever 40
Two Poems after Ovid 41
Yellow Dress 43
Cured 44
Western City 45
Botany Notes 47
No Child Will Choose It 48
Last Photo 49
Drowning in Bosporus 50

III

Gossip 53
The Shoes 54
Garden of Meats 55
What Children do in the Ravine 57
Wrought 58
Market 61
Blanca 62
Frozen Charlotte 63
The Body's Luck 65
Mumbletypeg 67
Lost Jockey 68

I

THE DEADLY POPPY FIELD

Their odor so powerful that anyone who breathes it
        sleeps within a ring of silken tents and is
innocent as water, as petals on roads of poplars
        with syrup-sky for pale distance, as milkmaid dreams
of pollen skirts among the clover. Cropper & tilled,
        spent sap of the body's best memory, this—
Sleepyhead, my poppy-milk, o field of deadly flowers:
        I know dark from bright & milk from white
in hawthorne-flower; I know milk from honey.
        Would you have drunk the offered cup
just to sleep forever in the trembling grass?
        Ruination and regret, I would have drunk it
bitter grain & bitter sleep, if you'd lay down.

CABEZÓN

I see you shuffle up Washington Street
whenever I am driving much too fast:
you, chub & bug-eyed, jaw like a loaf
hands in your pockets, a smoke dangling slack
from the slit of your pumpkin mouth;
humped over like the eel-man or geek,
the dummy paid to sweep out gutters,

drown the cats. Where are you going now?
Though someday you'll turn your gaze
upon my shadow in this tinted glass
I know for now you only look ahead
at sidewalks cracked & paved with trash
& what are you slouching toward—knee-locked,
hippity, a hitch in your zombie walk, Bighead?

PHOTOGRAPH IN A MONTANA BAR

When you finally decipher the image, made by some miracle
inside the camera's chamber and your eyes adjust to what light is
left and not opaque with smoke or flame-white dust, you'll see

the photograph is not a random pile of bones, nor even
an elk's corpse or luckless cow naturally slaughtered, but
a tangle of moose and hunter, bones picked nearly clean

though still darker than the snow they lie in with faces near
enough to whisper; knuckles resting on the long skull and
here & there ribbons of hide or cloth; when you see the rifle

twisted at the frame's edge, the very hieroglyph of mishap, and
know that in spring weeds will cover it & twist rampant through
arches of rib with rings of flowers surrounding all, the trick is

not just to marvel at the manner of this death but to imagine
stepping from hemlock to a clearing into the gold
& shaking autumn light with this embrace a few seconds away.

FROM VACANT LOTS, FLOWERS . . .

Tropic and vernal and veined as flesh, bursting
out of vacant lots, flowers scattered over the hot streets;
all those sharp cars glazed with petals

and a gritty shine of seed; in Miami
vines grew even from the stone walls
each vetch & tendril quivering toward the rain

everything a hungry mouth—oh, I knew what it was
when my breasts leaked in sympathy
when the roots of my bad tooth stirred

and blossomed into pain, I recognized that grasp
like bulbs struggling from earth
as I sat mute and harmless at the pool

with the baby and my fat mother-arms, awake
every hour trembling in the aura of her sleep, the night
humid with marshes of mangrove and strangler

all pulled into mud by the weight of their opulence:
that weed-green body, that swamp of hollow stems
whose breath becomes the rich air of this world.

HUMBUG

When I think of you I think of hucksters
on the midway calling promises against the dark;
you & your bon mot, your slick tongue, your gaff.

I think of the oracles loosing their wars,
ventriloquists speaking for alien saviors
(but how the eyes move, the mouth opens!)

Pull back the curtain. Among silver wires
and pulleys, the balloon again poised for escape—
& what about my heart my brains my home?

We wipe tears with coat-sleeve, you depart
for another gig. Tripe-wife, mango, humbug:
think of me and life seems greener than it is.

ROOSTER SHADOW

It's not by chance that as this house returns to rot,
the outer rooms fill up with feathers: jackdaw
and grackle black, grit-colored slivers of sparrow
or finch that grub for crumbs on every sidewalk.

Don't be fooled by thrash or rapture:
a bird is only vitriol, a lizard's foot,
gristle and a sack of stones, diviner of nothing
but endings. If you doubt it, think of cockfights

or starlings' pulse against the rain-wet glass
each Spring returning to shock you
with darkness like blood in the yolk. Spurious, plagiarist—
amid thick leaves I saw the wink of black eyes
waiting in dark pines, the snow-broken greenhouse.

On my stairs there is a rooster's shadow.
Nights the rafters host a storm of chatter, the breeze
of a thousand wings, but in the morning
dirty legions rise silent from one winter's tree.

COTTON & TURNIP

I freely confess my particular indisposition to be moved by [vegetables] . . . often accounted Prodigies.

—Cotton Mather

When Heaven spoke through nature any cabbage
might show a rupture in the Human sphere.
That stalk whose puny root should not have held it
Was an omen for the rot of souls, a Prodigy of sin
& Divination—& Still you say the blood is on us!
Friends, it was not Salem's first ominous Turnip,
Nor the first trespass He answered with excess—
Did you think all dead in the flood had equally sinned?
Goody Parker, Becky Nurse & Wilmott Reed.
Martha hanged & Giles stoned for standing mute,
Sarah Wilds, Sarah Good. As the powers of air
Leave barren the world, the righteous will perish,
Some few, among the wicked. Though good wheat's lost
When pestilence descends, you burn the field.

AGAIN, THE DONKEY

Quince: Bless thee Bottom . . . thou art translated!

Sometimes although I want to speak
exultant but calmly of deep clover
& clean straw or my sweetest late

encroachment upon the fields at dusk,
instead this bray utters itself
broken & ardent: pulled from my lips

like this—echoing others all over Noon
and igniting in turn,
more awful songs of lust & contrition.

≈

Obstinate no word for it: *mulish*
Lip poked out, heels in. Say it.

Say the shape of a mule's hoof
parodies the horse's highstep:

too wide at the bottom, off balance
as opposite parents; yes, call me

brassmouth; forget my equine side, but
spurious, ignoble I refuse.

≈

At night we browse the province of an empty market
& hustle through dark alleys with our suitors' recompense,

but in the vacant plaza I am king:
starving hounds flinch before my hoofs
and the white pigeon panics.

Velvet-lipped & long of tooth, wire-whiskered—
in the dark I sing
so they will hear that I am not afraid.

TRAIN

Cheyenne 1950

In some versions of your story the switchman turned
in time to see the *Century* slip its hold, escape

the brakes & start down Sherman Hill unmanned.
In some the engine ghosts away without a glance

one hundred tons of iron racing toward Cheyenne
with just the pistons rumbling, whistleless,

shaking the ground, wheels a blur by the first turn:
she never jumped the tracks but ate the distance, flashing

like a long black casket, passing like the armored
hoards of empire or some plague just missing your house;

sometimes at a safe distance, sometimes so close
the rush blew off your hat & sometimes it was more

like a river that never swerved but kept to its task
while the guessed smash-end of this took shape

in your mind even then, I suspect, as a great tale
of witnessed catastrophe, of voluptuous & certain

destruction: what you saw and were spared; a tale
with extravagant & shifting details; one end to it

accentuates the bloom of light at impact
with an empty switcher in the yards & one

highlights the rain of iron. In one the boiling water
reached the ground but in another hissed, trapped

as vapor in the air, atom-bright and mingling
with the useless squeal of radios, before it disappeared.

SCENT

In spring the moths left dust-brown smears on windows
& made you living halos in the yard,
loathful, mindless, cleaving to screens—
another today, here on the floor, drags its dull wings
like a heavy cloak, this close to death & still love-drunk
drawn by pheromones that your skin took up
when your job was setting moth traps in the woods.

They'd said it stays until you sweat the last drop out—
this language that your cells still speak, without
knowing it, to Heterocera, the clouds, legions
of frantic iridescence, of miller-dust
of compound eye & ocellus, each trembling cell
a vision of what will never brook refusal
but keeps on beating & beating at the door.

HANGMAN

Draw your gallows. Ready the noose for my shorn ring.
I have seen daguerreotypes of women hanging

under hoods, like flowers black on broken stems
dark skirts spread like bells before a sea of louts,

the treeless street. Bring me to the trapdoor's brink.
Do you think I fear the arm or leg you draw for every letter

missed of cypress, mammon, Bwana? I know that alphabet
by now & though I hate the words proceeding

from your pallid lips, I am thinking now of prairie wind,
clear air between the shanty slants; a beautiful

& emptied space. I'll step off. Watch this.

PHOTO OF PASTEUR

Pestilence his coin: this glaring Frenchman,
sixty-four with tie askew
berating his assistant Emile Roux—arrogant, brash

he put his head into the circlets of poison
entered willingly chapels of bacilli
inhabited also fully the sadness of certain hours

dearest Marie so they will all die, our dear children
waited long moments for the sheep
to rise from Rossignol's pasture & stumble

from dawn fog & the scourge of charbon (but cried
from the train: *So, men of little faith!*)
Up to his neck in beet juice & the favor of chance

with a crookneck flask, the man who, attending a lecture
on childbed fever at the Paris Academy
sprung up impatient, shouting—

then drew for them in chalk the streptococcus:
a string of bead he'd seen shine under the lens
like the eggs of a toad painted scarlet.

ON TWO PAINTINGS BY NARCISSE VIRGIL DIAZ DE LA PEÑA

First, a half-tame summer field and oaks
that frame a pond so thick with life it sinks the light

into a swarm of yellow seed.
Then crouching near the edge, a woman's shape
in shade, a pool of strokes

black as root or rot.
Even if she's just a painter's ghost

the spot his brush returned to
once you've seen her she eclipses
all the rest: the parceled farms implied beyond

the fringe of trees, the tidy bails and sheep.
There's something damp about her, something chill

& secret; you think about a child,
a slave or mistress, someone
down among the sodden leaves

until you see her in the second painting
a muddy smear again, yet unmistakably

a woman, and recognize the body
in the forest, where fallen trees
make giant graves; the one in hophorn

or old furrows, in water and shade
in roots becoming soil, in empty stems

becoming mist when evening takes
the ruined field back. There: belly a pool,
feet of mushrooms, face of moss.

VARICOSE

What drew that blue map behind your right knee?
Was it the long hours spent
grading papers, legs crossed? Was it the baby?

Was it the miles run on sidewalks, concrete-strain
of twenty years? Or some implacable chromosome stamp
that bruises & blurs like an ink stain on crêpe?
Diffuse, *infirm*—dropped elastic or balding tire

or shells, saphena, floe china broken—
and consider the beauty of a knotted blue thread
or shallow stream pressing through a sludge of sand
(tributary: creek, or one who bears the cost);

vessel stretched thin, skin leaking its wine; words
coughed from the mouth after years—
oh the long years of patience—*enough enough*

VERTIGO

insomnia . . . a lingering metallic taste, euphoria—

If the medication wakes you early, you may reflect
more truly on the garden's ruin of late weeds among
black apples and the sunflowers' awaited surrender

that itself is chemical; in dawn's light you may know
that all around us pharmack mysteries are at work;
and reflect, not unhappily, that life is brief; no more

than the flaring, really, of Hydromedusa or light
from a luminous tide. You may sit and not cringe
remembering failures, swervings of will; dread

for now recedes before that brightness which attends
vertigo and leg-jitter, nail-flavor, nausea; it is
the body talking after all and now when morning comes

again crimson to the lawn toys' stirring; when
schoolbus doors part again with their enduring sigh
you will rouse yourself from laboratory dreams

of sourceless hallways, mortars, ancient jars;
but not of martyred mice or primates, remember
as every cell in the vine dies another kind is born,

nematode or snowflake, as here in a dawn garden
you may hear the highway's drone as oars in dark water
and calmly wait for winter, never caring if it comes.

GUNSLINGER

Easy to imagine him: young & newly dead,
face black with powder, shrugging into line
behind the other men killed for cattle, land,

by bad liquor, accident, some lynched
in this courtyard, all gone down into darkness
like so many black pegs on a roller organ,

each now dust in muslin winding
beneath a wooden cross; his rush towards slaughter
done. Here's another gun. Here's a blood-dipped fringe

& here's another corpse on tintype, propped up with his Colt's, the telltale
fly-black spot on his forehead, one eye half-shut.
In a trunk back East there's a picture of him living, this

distant cousin no one can put a name to
squinting at a garden party, head thrown back
as though he had already taken the shot.

ON PREFERRING RED OR BLACK DATES

Even his choice of red or black dates . . . will show you something of your lover's nature.

—Sayd Ibn-al-Shayk

I'll be sweetly locust-skinned if you'll be tart
when served unripe: spice or honey; sulfur, loam—
or I'll be sharp & you be sweet; forgetting

there are yellow dates, and purple dates,
forgetting everything but how the red dates taste
like meager shade, the fruit of thirst itself

& how black ones dipped in butter cloy like sin
until we loathe them—Habib, Al-Shayk
(in darkened rooms at noon, a moonlit roof)

would you be camel's milk or silver basin,
indigo or salt? Belled herds, or herdsmen's thirst
for bitter coffee thick with grains? If you'll be dunes

then I will be a short green season, or the sea
that deepens while our bones forget
this trance of flesh—O Speak, Kabir, don't

hover, thinking of the separate taste of each!
The gold tray is before you. Take your pick
of discontent, since you would tire of the chaste

& promised daughter or the whore; what
you want lives in a memory, just choose:
root or fruit, goats or sheep, here or there, this

or that—you don't have all day, al-Shayk.
There is no riddle but this mystery of flesh,
sweeter water from a dreamed oasis—

II

ZUCKERMAN'S DAUGHTER

Would she glance up subjugate as one
on the day of execution
would she look up to you would she

stray from the flock in her opulence
so vast so green so rich a field
would she stay or would she stray

would the gentlemen-farmers
would the pig farmers the onion farmers

would they belly up would they put up pay up
would they shut up
& would the luckless husbands

trade ale for a dancing lesson
Listen—
which of us littered the landscape with souls

which of us vanished in ether?
But this is a true story was there
one who drew a permanent compass

was there one who wanted
to take her apart kernel & core
bone & soul, seam & length of skin

was there one who closed the door
said How would it be
if nobody knew what went on in this room

was there a song were there songs
she's a swoon I moon her
a beautiful dusk and I must her

still waiting & dropped down like seed
was there one who put breath in the river
were there songs between us was it always so

SONNET FOR AN EARLY THAW

While the sky turns towards its long dusk
we scramble down the crumbling bank
toward the canal to watch the ravens
rise and slowly quarrel, catcall—

The cattails have long surrendered their beds.
Will you speak to me sometimes?
This is the only river I have ever known

this trickle stagnant in summer and now,
now that paper hearts adorn the windows
now winter has entered the marrow of bricks
it is still no river, and you are not here, though

Clapper travels every Bell's iron circle
and somewhere quarries fill & empty
with the early thaw: icy, dark and starless.

MOTHER AS A HOUSE

This is the house you will always live in:
the house whose windows have a different face
each time you look: amused and certain

or tearful, outraged into silence, mad;
a hint of highball mirth in slanting shades,
that flap of siding like a little tic.

Light will never fill the rooms or move the dust
in tides among the bedrid pots;
chock-full and locked up tight, this house:

crawl space, attic door, fulsome clump of spruce,
it stands against the hills, a stark
& awful shack but o you love your house

this house you have always lived in;
shuttered, dreaming, parsed as puzzles
its thin-lipped children done in cross-stitch

& dustbowl ghost inside a sphere of brass.
This is the house you will always live in
even when the roof caves in and windows smash

no ceiling, no curtain will keep the rain off you.
Every hall this narrow hallway,
every garden riven by this path.

CROUP

Rise again to start the shower, start the kettle, fill the house with steam.

Soak a sugar cube in whiskey, boil an onion for the churchyard cough, for the night cough, grained, rib-shaking, for fear rich again between rilled breaths,

the bleat of pink that can't grasp air. Start a kettle. Start the kitchen door astir on its swing hasp

(& all the pages curling yellow-up, the frames forever stained)

while the child, flushed & coughing dreams of *eating plums, fat plums bleeding pink in drifts* of snow; the kettle screams

& her breath smells of something pursed and sour. You want to shake her body into breathing. You want to smooth the fever from her palms and hot face; stop

the lungs the urgent heart from balking *in her dream one plum has no pit just a tiny scroll with camels palms & turbaned men, labyrinths of ribbon script*

in a trill of lymph & creaking door, in tides of steam that curl like rind against cold glass; *and now there is a puddle in the drifts, a puddle bright with fish* wondering

will the vapor save us? Will the slice of light grow narrow?

But when dawn comes breath finds a purchase. *When star mouths catch upon the lip of breath*

when streetlights fade like poppy heads and brake lights stain the droplets red, shut the kettle off. Crack the window. Steam will find its own way out.

THE COCKFIGHT

after Patrick Fermor

Rouge fell dead before L'Homme aux Surprises
upon the square of beaten earth, a hole
between his breast & neck, bristles limp
and mad remaining eye gone glazed. When the victor

climbed the corpse & spread his wings
and crowed—a long triumphant crow, we fled
from that plank court into a rainy street
winnings in our hands. Now, remembering

an awful wound that didn't bleed, the other,
pecked-out eye; remembering the greasy bills
sailing to & fro across the ring, would you
go back beneath that roof of rotting fronds

to the plumage, spur and fury-shaken dust;
would you return to watch them sail
into the air claw to claw & hang there, heraldic
two blood suns with beating wings;

or to see the trainer who filled his own mouth
with water & pressed the bird to his lips:
wetting each feather so it should cling
and afford no hold to the enemy?

FEVER

Blame yourself when you wake shaking the bed:
melancholic, wet & menaced by chairs;
the pulse in your temple a shutter in storms.
There's only you to blame for skipping your pills
for traveling the damp side of high roads at dusk:
you who went deep into the green rice fields
& into the realm of the fields' winged queens.
So there was a heron that covered the sun.
So there were frogs & a ribbon-bright snake.
Perhaps you wanted to drift the backwater
of your sickroom, oarless in the tangled shade?
Now every night your sheets are a river
& the song of the winnower sung in your bones.

TWO POEMS AFTER OVID

in a moment she was seen and loved and taken—

in a moment I was past the roots' last reach
—*cold hands on my face*—past seam & cinder-slag
and the reeking dark cradles of stars.

Up there the field might blossom into flame;
blight might stink like bloodshot eggs, but I
am just another bead of spawn gone down,

another slant of shade for evening's husk.
Do you use the word *ravished*? Do you still imagine
flesh rent by thunder, the breath of a swan,

a ram's brute advances; or do you recognize
his frail caress, now oxen drag their broken plows,
now turnips are skulls in the earth?

and [Ceres] beat her breast & tore her hair. Where is she?

In the deep seam. In sulfur. In the marrow,
dust, onion-rustle, beetleskin and cache of seed—

Lost calf in a dreamy well:
Bawling. Then quiet. Here I have
no lips no mouth no tongue to speak with

Lost daughter who the mothers call down rows of days—

I forget the upper air. I drink the dirt
will you find me

when winter wants its draught of pollen
when the plow is crossed with rust
will you push the earth aside

YELLOW DRESS

Port-au-Prince

Girl on a heap of street sweepings high
as a pyre, laid on snarled wire & dented rim.
Girl set down among the wrung-out hides.
A girl who was coming from church. It is late
Sunday afternoon. *Was it a seizure? Is it*
destiny or bad luck we should fear? Weak heart
or swerving taxi? In Tet Bef by the dirty ocean
thousands crush past her without pausing
at the shrine of her splayed limbs; brilliance
like the flesh of lilies sprouting from the pummeled cane.
Is it possible to be lighthearted, hours later?
Days? To forget the yellow dress?
I am waiting for her mother to find her, still
wearing one white spotless glove (*where is the other?*),
my idle taxi level with her unbruised arm,
her fingers just curling like petals of a fallen flower
and how did it end? Let someone have gathered her up
before the stars assembled coldly overhead:
her dress brighter than gold, crocus, the yolk of an egg
her face covered like the bride of a god; let them
have found her & borne her through the traffic's clamor
veiled with a stranger's handkerchief.

CURED

Mansoor's shop smells of everything
cured & exotic—hides embroidered red,

silk nests of black eggs blown unbroken;
tiny boxes carved of camel's hoof,

hinges filled with sand; crumbling rams' horns,
everything rescued from random rot

& changed to something people want. So
I say leukemia is a flower—a tiny white

blossom in the blood, lush as phlox
tranquil as scent on a silk dress.

Sarcoma is gem, hard as zircon
cold but rich with promise; Metastatis

is reached through prayer & meditation
and lymphoma the rare weather

That created Venus—made her rise
from the sea foam, pink as a new infant,
while grateful crabs applauded from the shore.

WESTERN CITY

That glimmer is not the dead rising from their shattered cars,
or, corpse-stiff, stumbling from ditches,

but a flickering jack-light, an antler or shimmer of bone
from the river's cradle: Rio Puerco, strata of dark sand

ash, transfigured stars, starved cattle's trench
where the dead sip, with no woods

or green weeds to conceal them:
Citizens of an indifferent wind; O modest dead, speechless,

unheeded warnings to those who come thinking
this climate some proof of election or change:

Even now they are coming, even now
holding maps up to study the distance

the city dreamed out of darkness
squinting from nine-mile hill at the gridlines;

a pageant arrival to burn off the past.
Who doesn't wish to fall like a comet

into the future, to vanish in sparks and effulgence of light?
Here we hide bodies in plain sight: all tombs

should be of air, gully or train-bed, barren fields
where houses proceed from a treeless landscape, this

imagined city, inelegant city—but discrete
in the block of its state, standing Oz-like on the flatland

Even the ghosts rise up to it—
an island surrounded by blizzards of darkness.

BOTANY NOTES

Improbable love song scribbled on the lines of a narrow spiral:
buds acute, buds blood-red, buds silky all over, buds
sketched beside smears of his blood which is honey to chiggers

& ticks, his skin always livid, nicked & bitten: *the word the blood*
all this because he would rather work in the forest than any
coffee-reeking office; this ink that anchors knowledge on a rain-

warped page: *love, ink, memory* of each brown, gray, green piece of the
universe, the swath of Carolina woods, bug-abundant early,
brambled, burrowed, hazy with chill sunlight & spiderweb, semis

roaring by in a shudder of trunks, all this pinned to the eye
of singing noon; the stooping grass, the parceled orchard run
to dismal & the cellar filled with weeds, the hunk of rusted

car, but this song is for the buds in spring: solitary, clothed in scales
drooping, blue-black, yellow; buds downy, dark with whitish
pubescence; close-up—no, closer. Buds sweet. Heavy-headed.

Buds that never winter shut. Buds then flowers then dry petals
scattered in the breath of heat; all that opened like secrets
to his ink, humble; buds with slippery, nearly black inner bark.

NO CHILD WILL CHOOSE IT

Who would pick him over zebras
or the pig, sun-yellow with a racy grin?
Green-saddled & set between a white steed

crowned with roses and the lover's bench,
the rooster with one scaled foot drawn up
looks at first like crockery, eye bright

but dead flat, feathers a bric-a-brac insult.
The others seem copied at least
from something inspired: the ram's ham

scrotum & the mermaid flecked
with beaten froth; each prancing horse alive
in plastic, alive with tendons, cruel nostril, knee—

all pulling hard against the halter.
The cock's the only one not poised to move;
puppet out of Kansas with a sulfur gaze,

profile watching for locust.
Even under tiny lights that wink like stars,
or deafened by the organ's crash, no child

will choose it; up close coarse-skinned as you'd think:
red feathers flame on a dark tail's landscape,
some war fire set on a massacre hill.

LAST PHOTO

The photo of my mother bald
looks more like her than any other:
I think because it's often hair the camera
fails, makes it flat, too dark or lumpy—
set on solid as an ugly hat.

Not this photo. My mother's head is neat
and pleasing as the egg an artist draws
to make a perfect head; her brow unlined
and high with eyebrows painted on: fake,
dramatic, brave. Her smile pulled sideways
is a challenge to approaching absence—the lips
and eyebrows say: I know the reason
for this photo of me, all dressed in black
before a bone-white wall. Go ahead and take it.

DROWNING IN BOSPORUS

From my father's burning house they took me
to bed in the green river's indolent depth.
When they held my face in the water I asked
what to leave them, the mob & the soldiers,
what proof of my loathing, what lingering blight?

In their cart down the plague roads
to this river from the leper's house they took me
that day crowds were lethargic & parted before us
while I wished for a cradle of weeds to receive me
a bower of rushes, an altar of cane—

From the stew they brought me, from the brothel
again to the River of Venus, the River of fevers:
low between dry fields, my path of green sand,
the ribboning tides & the murderous water
I learned at last to drink deep, and go under.

GOSSIP

—Didn't you know water would be the end of me?

See what you have done, she said.
For a moment we were both amazed
as she began to ebb away
behind her eye patch, pointed hat—*O*
I have been wicked in my day, she said
but she was melting: tooth & palate,
half-moon chin, so it might have been
I had been tricky in my day—meaning
I suppose no other charm like salt
in churns or iron's kiss had yet deterred her.
I thought I heard *I never thought*
a girl like you could end my wicked deeds;
it might have been *could send me wicked dreams*
or *end by tickling me* or even
bend my wicker seams—
I drew another bucket then
to wash away the mess for there
was not a fluent moment left; it was
the end & her last words were bubbles
in a rush of suds. *You bitch you murdered me*
is surely what she meant to say
but all's mixed up in history now
(*a girl some shoes my wicked tricks*);
& water cleans whatever deeds invent.

THE SHOES

Although interpreted by some as symbolic menstruation
they were really silver, transformed to ruby for the
Technicolor screen.

They inspired in their owners an unwholesome attachment
trod roads of fire in the ancient story

continued the tradition of magic shoes and flight
(though provoked would stretch & hang flaccid, grotesquely)

yearned secretly towards whoever desired them
adventured with the oilcan in pathless fields

mornings always compassed West
were more powerful than the golden cap and Glinda's kiss
together—& believe me

were so singularly flamboyant, mysterious, and possessed
other powers never discovered
were feared, restored silence

in any room, had long traced the expectancy in every stolen
glance, and still

had no heart to remain with us. Will answer no prayer.

GARDEN OF MEATS

All text is lost, but illustrations left
suggest these flowers lived on meat
and, though largely brainless—dopey-eyed

with sweeping lashes on their flytrap heads—
were still rapacious, serpentine
above the scalloped farmers; goodwives

garnished with an upturned rib.
What's not shown is how the five
escaped from their prisons of vine

(the Tinman axeless, the Scarecrow,
as usual, disemboweled & helpless).
We don't know anything about it, really:

why one cabbage-headed shrub
behind the Lion seems to weep or grimace;
how much food was captured

& how much grown from seed;
whether babies slung & pantried
in those peapod cradles

slept through death; whether
their souls became cherubs
in vegetable churches, luminous

& opulent beneath the leaves, or even
why L. Frank Baum—who, my text assures me
was *so fond of flowers*—

wrote about so many deadly plants, and not just these;
whether the author sat on the porch
on cool evenings listening to the breath

of fields, watching arms of wisteria
wrap the iron trellis; whether or not
this, too, is a story of innocence.

WHAT CHILDREN DO IN THE RAVINE

or garden shed or greenhouse, in eucalyptus huts
or cellars where stray cats squeeze out their young
is no business of ours; we'll never remember
any spells or how our warnings flap as fraying rafters.
The children have left the house. They scramble
down a waterfall of rocks to weeds and peed-in sand
to put caught bees to bed in glass, scrawl maps,
light matches in a cave of thorns, or swear

allegiance to the darkness while their voices grow
so faint we must follow the trail of their play
as it dissolves, like moths on water; so faint
that I will make an offering of momentary fear
to the hole that gapes toothless and blooming:
I am only another mother calling through the flaming dusk.
Sometimes the children launch a jar into the farthest rocks
and watch the bees like souls enraged, escaping—

WROUGHT

There are words for the hours girls spent
obedient to the needle, by candle & gaslight:
true stitch, rococo stitch, gusset, seam & band—

Girls called Hannah, Frances, Ruth & Sarah
sat by sickbeds, salts clutched in the still hand:

O Christ permit thy gracious name to stand
As the first efforts of an infant's hand—

Plain & Fancy, for Collar or Cuff.
For the new bride white, rice & Eyelet.
Feather stitching for the edge of pantalets,
or the gold-skeined tips of flowers.

·

Here is one by Frances Bassford, 1841
whose alphabet sits tight as type
on the first line, before it comes undone:

Stitch of Madness, Stitch of Palsy, Stitch of Failing Sight

letters flattened,
like vowels unspooling from deaf speech,
long & bleating, that yowl of diphthong,
perceived as agony, though I likely

mispronounce this stitch—

o trembling hand shaking itself out of laburnum borders!

.

Girls wrought these who at other times were dreaming
of tall grass, dreaming
of the fiddler's pale son, of falling water—

This work was done by Ruth Body she hated every stitch

Girls looking into rain barrels at quivering reflections
even as our faces look back from museum glass.

And behind us ceiling lights & gleaming tiles rush
to meet as corn rows in the distance.

Like a crane or a swallow I did chatter, I did mourn—

.

Under blazing sky
wide the locust road its light unwavering
under haste & hurt & hoary love,
under imperfect attention
among the green corn silk untangling. . . .

.

But the canvas gives no privacies, no silence
no ordure, no rapture—

Their faces are no faces, long covered in darkness.

Spool & Thread, hoop & frame; the task remains:

forget not thy helpless infancy
letters closed like houses from the rain
forget not that, forget not this
canvas pliable but still too strong to rip
Scythe, cherry blossom, schoolhouse, winter wheat—

MARKET

Fat hearts swing from the butcher's hook,
weeping their blood into dust.
Some drops are borne away on skin, on shoes

or hems of gauze while vendors sing *how soft*
my fleece and cheap and you, oblivious,
up to your elbows in grave swag and rust

paw through the piles without buying.
o sir put your lips to this silk
You are the one who wades hip-deep in surf

while the best shells bide in the belly of swell.
So sweet the flesh of my black dates!
You are the one who runs to buy onions

only when the market tarps start down.
For what would you open your purse?
but come don't turn away don't snub my salt

Come choose a hide, a papaya.
Trade your coin for this bottle
blown bright by my breath, for this jar of souls

just buy it, you goiter, poor miser this silver
this tasket, this splinter, this lazuli eye:
all worth it, all waiting long years for your price.

BLANCA

She used to make him eggs with flowers.
Wild white bulbs, pearl & ivory blossoms
beetle and night's moth-mated buds
that opened in the quick exchange of liquid
yolk for omelet. Now when he hears her name

he sees those creamy flowers unfolding
sour & reluctant among fiddleheads or flame
softening into fragrant oily slips
tangy secret papers, fortunes. And knows
for this one memory there are a thousand

others: moments unsavored, eaten by time,
moments deflowered, bolted, lost & squandered
now faint as a spent field, memory of dark
canopy, cryptic as the alphabet of wasps.

FROZEN CHARLOTTE

They appear in every city's iron-dark
& tainted cellar soil, white as bone
blank as noon, feet & tiny hands unearthed

by 'dozer jaws. Some come whole,
propped sideways in the dirt
or hidden in a small red shoe.

When machines recede we fill our pockets
with dolls and shards of dolls
that never moved: jointless

naked, prim & plump-thighed mummies,
at tea parties leaning stiff on chairs—
Years took off the paint

and settled in their molded hair.
They come with rust
in the unglazed bisque of belly

or behind a dimpled knee
from slaughterlots & dirty fields
from underneath the eyeless

long-abandoned factories
where women lost their sight
to inkle looms—& like their children

we imagine coal-smudged, darkly clad
& joyless, these ugly dolls
are sullen even at their rescue,

colic babies still refusing food;
bribes paid with a rusty coin:
unmourned and the dullest of corpses

we long ago tired of finding, but tireless machines
keep turning up dirt
& showing stillborn faces to the light.

THE BODY'S LUCK

Back then, twin bunches of lymph twitching
in the throat's crypt were a mystery,
mine inflamed, always painful: nights on the sick couch
and spoonfuls of a thick pink liquid.
Now we know they bear the T-cells that protect
against colds, innumerable cancers, ills—

If hypochondria is loss of faith in the body's luck
mine began the day they said *You won't miss them.*
But I felt gypped, and ignored the unctuous nurses,
knowing tonsils weren't the last thing I would lose to them
and suspecting too
that there would be no trades, much less rewards.

At the optic shop they lulled me, first
with dim lights, a spoon on the eye and pictures
of air balloons in Western skies
before they shocked me with the inside of my retina
that sad planet, that blood and yellow atlas
where mitochondria and air bubbles cruise

like Greyhounds on wet road. Then the charts:
oppressive, gnashed as barbed wire, *read the last line*
you can see (of broiled commas, knots); the doctor
leaning close with his beautiful words
myopia, astigmatism, he said, and then *with age*
your eyesight will surely get worse. . . .

·

More proof of my body's failing: a back tooth
cracked clean as an ice cube in hot water.
The root canal was just a Valium haze. What was bad
was when they ground that dead tooth down
and bits of it flew out of my mouth like crumbs
of shattered china—I fear

the teeth of the old, all that silver and decay
proceeding from the gums, yes, longer every year;
teeth which my teeth are now becoming,
& now this new one, porcelain, sturdy as plumbing
aches as the others do at cold or sweets
though they promised it would have no feeling.

·

A line blue and unequivocal, minimal letter:
the body's announcement of occupancy.
The waiting room was garden-bright
and full of pamphlets, lists, instructions,
as though I'd entered a new profession.

Even the pink poster fetus
seemed to wink its salamander eye
indulgently from the depths of some ancient
impersonal knowledge. The other women, too,
looked knowing and complaisant when I entered.

Returning to a house I'd long ago forgotten—
Enter. Welcome to our realm, the body.

MUMBLETYPEG

Don't aim too straight but don't throw fancy either;
just spit for luck and trust the flash of sun
to warm the blade before it hits the dirt.
You'd know the antler handle in your sleep
as you know its lightning shape in air: that glint
of sickle so much sharper having slipped
your grasp—and landing better, always,
knee-tossed, pitched from heel. But none of that
until there's thaw enough to hold your point:
you want to see it stick, then come out clean.
Miss the circle and a knife's no gift
but in this season hoops won't do nor marbles
in spring the force that binds all blistered hands
invites you: come stand and draw your blade.

LOST JOCKEY

Your mare's neck living iron when she breaks the fence—
guests scattered; cakes, tea-trays shattered, windows;
& meets the avenue with just the merest stumble

(a frantic blast of horns, drivers swerving); let them
call it a fraud now, this thunder through all
imaginable silence: prayer or meditation

penmanship lesson; treaties broken
bets off, houses torn like paper in your wake.
You meanwhile are hanging on, chin to saddle, slant

as an accent *grave*, your teeth rattled in a cup of skull
& see how the crowds stand up as you pass,
rise shouting like a Roman legion

from the wreckage with nowhere
to send complaints, because you are really
going this time, like gone, & all the way.

SOME PREVIOUS TITLES IN THE CARNEGIE MELLON POETRY SERIES: 2000-2006

2000

Small Boat with Oars of Different Size, Thom Ward
Post Meridian, Mary Ruefle
Hierarchies of Rue, Roger Sauls
Constant Longing, Dennis Sampson
Mortal Education, Joyce Peseroff
How Things Are, James Richardson
Years Later, Gregory Djanikian
On the Waterbed They Sank to Their Own Levels, Sarah Rosenblatt
Blue Jesus, Jim Daniels
Winter Morning Walks: 100 Postcards to Jim Harrison, Ted Kooser

2001

The Deepest Part of the River, Mekeel McBride
The Origin of Green, T. Alan Broughton
Day Moon, Jon Anderson
Glacier Wine, Maura Stanton
Earthly, Michael McFee
Lovers in the Used World, Gillian Conoley
Sex Lives of the Poor and Obscure, David Schloss
Voyages in English, Dara Wier
Quarters, James Harms
Mastodon, 80% Complete, Jonathan Johnson
Ten Thousand Good Mornings, James Reiss
The World's Last Night, Margot Schilpp

2002

Among the Musk Ox People, Mary Ruefle
The Memphis Letters, Jay Meek
What it Wasn't, Laura Kasischke
The Finger Bone, Kevin Prufer
The Late World, Arthur Smith
Slow Risen Among the Smoke Trees, Elizabeth Kirschner
Keeping Time, Suzanne Cleary
Astronaut, Brian Henry

2003

Imitation of Life, Allison Joseph
A Place Made of Starlight, Peter Cooley
The Mastery Impulse, Ricardo Pau-Llosa
Except for One Obscene Brushstroke, Dzvinia Orlowsky
Taking Down the Angel, Jeff Friedman
Casino of the Sun, Jerry Williams
Trouble, Mary Baine Campbell
Lives of Water, John Hoppenthaler

2004

Freeways and Aqueducts, James Harms
Tristimania, Mary Ruefle
Prague Winter, Richard Katrovas
Venus Examines Her Breast, Maureen Seaton
Trains in Winter, Jay Meek
The Women Who Loved Elvis All Their Lives, Fleda Brown
The Chronic Liar Buys a Canary, Elizabeth Edwards
Various Orbits, Thom Ward

2005

Laws of My Nature, Margot Schilpp
Things I Can't Tell You, Michael Dennis Browne
Renovation, Jeffrey Thomson
Sleeping Woman, Herbert Scott
Blindsight, Carol Hamilton
Fallen from a Chariot, Kevin Prufer
Needlegrass, Dennis Sampson
Bent to the Earth, Blas Manuel De Luna

2006
Burn the Field, Amy Beeder
Dog Star Delicatessen: New and Selected Poems 1979-2006, Mekeel McBride
The Sadness of Others, Hayan Charara
A Grammar to Waking, Nancy Eimers
Shinemaster, Michael McFee
Eastern Mountain Time, Joyce Peseroff
Dragging the Lake, Robert Thomas